For my best beloved Sister Mia
from
Julia Margaret Cameron.

With a blessing on
the New Years & the old.
July 7th 1863.

A
VICTORIAN ALBUM

Julia Margaret Cameron
and Her Circle

Introductory Essay by
Lord David Cecil

Edited by
Graham Ovenden

DA CAPO PRESS
NEW YORK 1975

Library of Congress Catalog Card No : 75–18728

ISBN : 0–306–70749–7

First American Edition 1975
by Da Capo Press

Published by Da Capo Press, Inc
A Subsidiary of Plenum Publishing Corporation
227 West 17th Street, New York, N.Y. 10011

Manufactured in Great Britain

CONTENTS

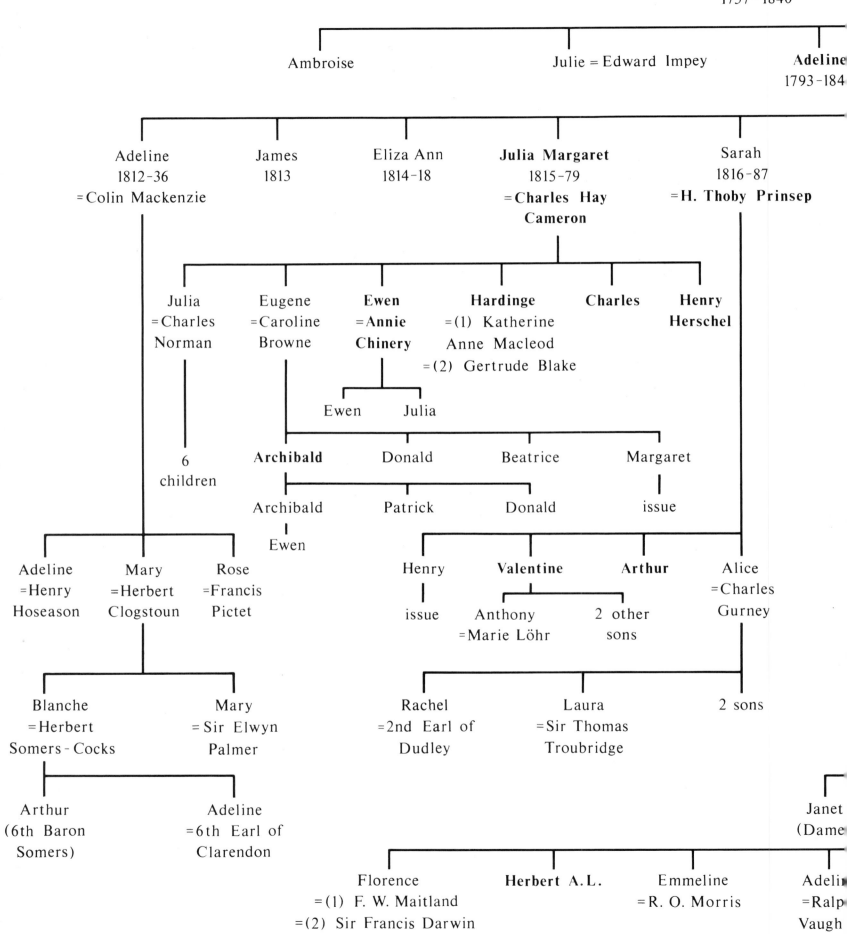

Ambroise Pierre Antoine
Chevalier de l'Étang
1757 - 1840

Ambroise   Julie = Edward Impey   **Adeline**
1793 - 184

Adeline	James	Eliza Ann	**Julia Margaret**	Sarah
1812-36	1813	1814-18	1815-79	1816-87
=Colin Mackenzie			=**Charles Hay**	=**H. Thoby Prinsep**
			Cameron	

Julia   Eugene   **Ewen**   **Hardinge**   **Charles**   **Henry**
=Charles   =Caroline   =**Annie**   =(1) Katherine   **Herschel**
Norman   Browne   **Chinery**   Anne Macleod
                                     =(2) Gertrude Blake

Ewen   Julia

Archibald   Donald   Beatrice   Margaret

6
children

Archibald   Patrick   Donald   issue

Ewen

Adeline	Mary	Rose	Henry	**Valentine**	**Arthur**	Alice
=Henry	=Herbert	=Francis				=Charles
Hoseason	Clogstoun	Pictet	issue	Anthony 2 other		Gurney
				=Marie Löhr sons		

Blanche	Mary	Rachel	Laura	2 sons
=Herbert	= Sir Elwyn	=2nd Earl of	=Sir Thomas	
Somers - Cocks	Palmer	Dudley	Troubridge	

Arthur   Adeline   Janet
(6th Baron   =6th Earl of   (Dame
Somers)   Clarendon

Florence	**Herbert A.L.**	Emmeline	Adeli
=(1) F. W. Maitland		=R. O. Morris	=Ralp
=(2) Sir Francis Darwin			Vaugh
			Willia

TREE

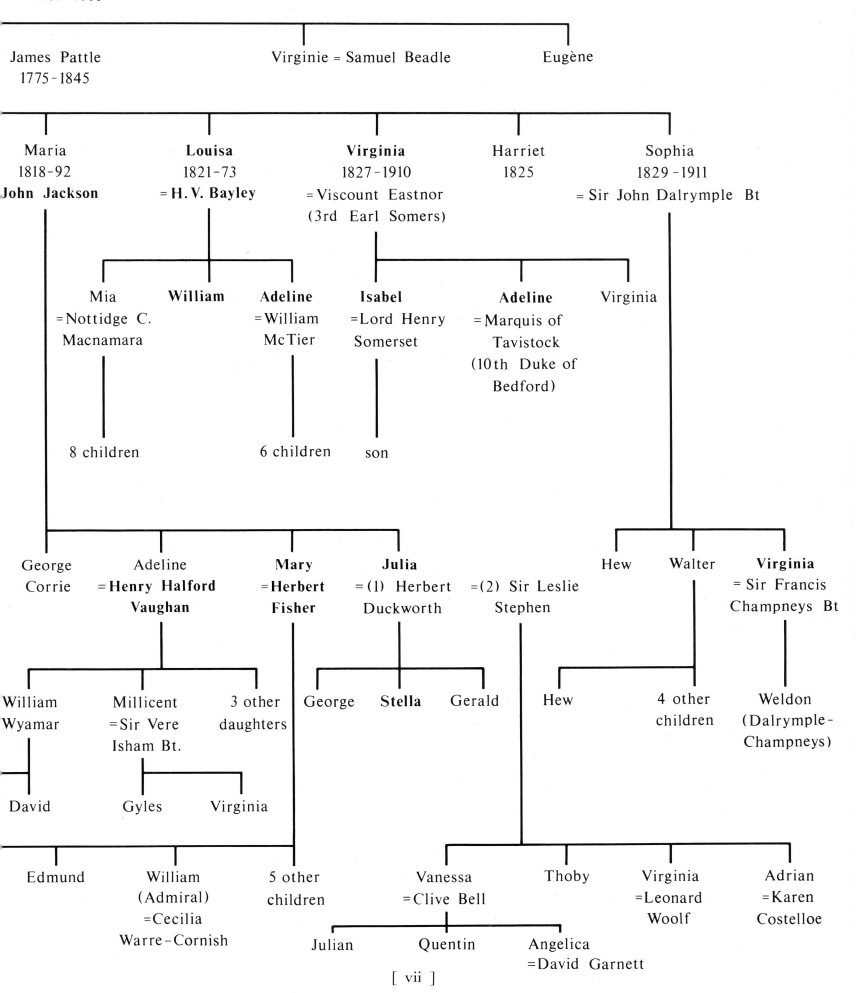

Thérèse Josephe Blin de Grincourt 1767–1866

James Pattle 1775–1845

Virginie = Samuel Beadle

Eugène

Maria 1818–92
John Jackson

Louisa 1821–73
= **H. V. Bayley**

Virginia 1827–1910
= Viscount Eastnor (3rd Earl Somers)

Harriet 1825

Sophia 1829–1911
= Sir John Dalrymple Bt

Mia = Nottidge C. Macnamara

William

Adeline = William McTier

Isabel = Lord Henry Somerset

Adeline = Marquis of Tavistock (10th Duke of Bedford)

Virginia

8 children

6 children

son

George Corrie

Adeline = **Henry Halford Vaughan**

Mary = **Herbert Fisher**

Julia = (1) Herbert Duckworth

= (2) Sir Leslie Stephen

Hew

Walter

Virginia = Sir Francis Champneys Bt

William Wyamar

Millicent = Sir Vere Isham Bt.

3 other daughters

George

Stella

Gerald

Hew

4 other children

Weldon (Dalrymple-Champneys)

David

Gyles

Virginia

Edmund

William (Admiral) = Cecilia Warre-Cornish

5 other children

Vanessa = Clive Bell

Thoby

Virginia = Leonard Woolf

Adrian = Karen Costelloe

Julian

Quentin

Angelica = David Garnett

[vii]

Introductory Essay

by LORD DAVID CECIL

I

ALBUMS of old photographs have a curious power to stir the historical imagination. There is nothing quite like these sallow faded prints for communicating the sense of a past period, the flavour and perfume of a vanished world. Consider this particular album. Collected by Julia Margaret Cameron as a present for her sister Mia Jackson, it seems to bring us into immediate personal touch with a whole social circle. It is also a distinguished manifestation of the photographer's art and the expression of a very remarkable personality.

The personality strikes one first. Julia Margaret was born in India in 1815, the daughter of an eminent Anglo-Indian jurist called James Pattle and his French wife Adeline de l'Étang. Julia and four of her sisters were later to become famous, some for beauty, some for talent, and all for formidable force of character. Julia herself was not a beauty – 'a woman of noble plainness' is the best that an enthusiastic friend can say of her appearance – but she was the most talented of her sisters, and the most forceful. This last quality showed itself early. In 1838 she married Charles Hay Cameron, twenty years older than herself and, like her father, an eminent Anglo-Indian jurist. She was passionately interested in her fellow human beings and, as soon as she was married, threw herself into social life both as guest and as hostess: with such energy and self-confidence that, while still under thirty, she was already the outstanding personality in Calcutta society.

This was not enough however to satisfy her aspirations. These were spiritual as well as social. As a young girl walking out with her sisters, she would suddenly fall on her knees in prayer: and she had grown up into a woman on fire with passionate dreams of the beautiful and ideal and always searching for a world in which they could be realised. Like a kindred spirit of a later period, Lady Ottoline Morrell, she desired 'a life lived on the same plane as poetry and as music'. This was not to be found among the mundane merchants and civil servants, who made up Calcutta society. However, in 1848 Charles Cameron retired from professional life to settle in England; Julia Cameron found the life she wanted there.

She was helped to do so by her sisters who had preceded her hither; and especially by her sister Sarah who was married to Thoby Prinsep. Sarah shared Julia's aspirations and had already set about achieving them. At Little Holland House in Kensington she had assembled around her a circle drawn from the most distinguished writers and artists of the day, including Tennyson, Browning, Millais, Rossetti, Burne-Jones and Watts. She had even persuaded

Watts to live in her house where, dressed picturesquely in a black velvet jacket and answering to the nickname of Signor, he occupied himself painting allegorical pictures expressive of lofty and uplifting sentiments.

Mrs Prinsep's was just the milieu that Mrs Cameron had been looking for: it satisfied both the social and the spiritual sides of her nature. She took every opportunity to cultivate friendships with persons noted for their power to open men's eyes to the ideal and the beautiful; and soon she was as friendly with Tennyson and the rest of them as her sister was. She became particularly intimate with Sir Henry Taylor, a handsome elderly poet, now forgotten but with a considerable reputation in his day. Mrs Cameron herself thought him a genius and took against any person who did not agree with her about this. Her relations with him were platonic: indeed she took pains to make a close friend of his wife, whom she showered with gifts of Eastern shawls, turquoise bracelets and ivory elephants; while, to win the heart of both wife and husband, she even had a room in their house redecorated according to her own taste without telling them. Understandably, they shrank a little from these energetic attentions. But Mrs Cameron persisted and soon they succumbed.

This was her effect on most people. The only recorded exceptions were Edward Lear and Lewis Carroll. Perhaps they found Mrs Cameron all too like the queer and overpowering figures depicted by them in *Alice in Wonderland* and the *Book of Nonsense Rhymes*. Indeed, stocky and heavy-faced, with a pair of expressive dark eyes and a harsh husky voice, Mrs Cameron was possessed of a personality in a high degree overwhelming. She was also eccentric. Dressed in defiance of fashion in flowing artistic draperies and bright-coloured Indian shawls, both usually in a state of disorder, she was liable to call on her friends unannounced at any hour of the day or night and was known to accompany a departing guest to the railway station bare-headed and carrying a cup of tea which she stirred, while going on talking animatedly on some artistic or literary topic. She was a great talker and the tone of her discourse – it is preserved for us in her voluminous letters – was relentlessly and rhapsodically romantic. Personal beauty especially inspired her to eloquence; as thus:

> Amongst the young Wives 'the Queen of Beauty' is Mrs Hambro, frolicsome and graceful as a kitten and having the form and eye of an antelope. She is tall and slender, not stately, and not seventeen – but quite able to make all daisies rosy and the ground she treads seems proud of her . . .
>
> Then her complexion (or rather her skin) is faultless – it is like the leaf of 'that consummate flower' the Magnolia – a flower which is, I think, so mysterious in its beauty as if it were the only thing left unsoiled and unspoiled from the garden of Eden. A flower a blind man would mistake for a fruit too rich, too good for Human Nature's daily food. We had a standard Magnolia tree in our garden at Sheen, and on a still summer night the moon would beam down upon those ripe rich vases, and they used to send forth a scent that made the soul faint with a sense of the luxury of the world of flowers. I always think that flowers tell as much of the bounty of God's love as the Firmament shows of His handiwork.

If Mrs Cameron often talked like this, it is not odd that Lear and Carroll found her company a strain. It must also have appealed to their sense of comedy: Mrs Cameron was in some respects a comic figure. But she was also an admirable one; warm-hearted, splendidly unconventional and so generous, that, struck by the beauty of Mary Ryan, an Irish beggar child she had met by chance on Putney Heath, she immediately adopted her and had her educated along with her own children. Contrary to the expectations and perhaps the hopes of Mrs Cameron's friends, this experiment was a success. Mary Ryan did, it is true, start her mature life in the modest role of parlour-maid. But her beauty soon got her a husband in a higher rank of life and she ended her days as Lady Cotton, the wife of a distinguished member of the Indian Civil Service.

[2]

In addition to her other virtues, Mrs Cameron also had an unusual power of enjoying herself and making other people do the same. From the time she arrived in England she found scope for this wherever she happened to find herself; but especially at Freshwater in the Isle of Wight. The Camerons settled there in 1860 in a pair of converted cottages bowered in roses and to which, in memory of happy days in the East, they gave the exotic name of Dimbola. Their main motive for choosing Freshwater as their home was to be near Tennyson who lived at Farringford; Mrs Cameron also thought it would be a stimulating home for her family. She wrote characteristically to Mrs Tennyson, 'How dear it will be for our children to grow and live happily together, playing mad pranks along the healthy lea!'

It was also an inspiring setting for her own mad pranks. For the next fifteen years, Dimbola, filled with a succession of distinguished guests, was the continuous scene of days spent in absorbing talk, poetic readings, romantic walks in wood or on down or by the murmuring sea waves, diversified in winter by improvised theatricals and lantern-lit revels and in summer by moonlit picnics and dances on the lawn. With those of her friends not at Dimbola, she kept in touch by means of frequent long and emphatic letters. When post time came, the gardener's boy scampered off with these letters to the post office. Often Mrs Cameron thought of a postscript after he had gone and sent the gardener with it hastening after the gardener's boy. Sometimes yet another postscript would occur to her and she herself would join in the pursuit, driving furiously in a donkey cart.

The acknowledged divinity ruling the Freshwater scene was Tennyson. All united to pay him homage and Mrs Cameron led the homage. Like other persons, Tennyson sometimes found her too much of a good thing. He grumbled when she wanted him to copy out a poem in his own hand as a present for one of her friends, or when she insisted on his going down to the beach to fling a garland of red and white flowers into the sea as a symbol that he, like the ancient doges of Venice, was a worthy bridegroom of the sea itself. He also refused to share her admiration for Sir Henry Taylor's beauty. 'I do not know what you mean by his extraordinary beauty, he has a smile like a fish!' All the same, Tennyson's pleasure in Mrs Cameron far outweighed his occasional irritation with her. He sunned himself in the warmth of her appreciation – after all it was agreeable to be treated as a god – and he was grateful for her kindness to his family. This could take curious and characteristic forms. Once when Mrs Cameron heard that the Tennysons' schoolboy son Hallam had been taken ill at Marlborough, she immediately sent him a parcel of presents, including a pair of purple and gold silk trousers and two Japanese tea-cups. These were exotic objects to appear amid the puritan rigours of a public-school sickroom. Still, their very strangeness may well have cheered Hallam up. They were an expression of Mrs Cameron's imaginative sense of pleasure and this was something that the Tennyson family responded to. Tennyson himself did so enthusiastically. He delighted in being taken by Mrs Cameron for midnight walks by the sea-shore and his majestic figure was to be seen at her dances, rotating slowly round the floor in a waltz. A sentence from a letter sums up his feeling for her: 'She is more wonderful than ever, with her wild beaming benevolence.'

Indeed life at Freshwater was startlingly, glamorously different from life in Calcutta. Even so, it did not at first wholly satisfy Mrs Cameron. From time to time she was visited by inexplicable fits of depression. The cause was frustration. Born an artist, possessed of a strong creative impulse, she had not found a mode through which to express it. Then in 1863 her married daughter presented her with a camera. It turned out to be the most important event in Mrs Cameron's life: for it meant that the artist in her had at last found a medium. Photography was a slow cumbersome process in those days, involving infinite patience and with the risk of failure at every turn. Mrs Cameron made nothing of all this. On fire with excitement, she turned a glazed chicken-house into a studio and a coal-hole into a dark-room and set to work. Within a year or two she was producing pictures which are still among the few masterpieces of photographic art.

[3]

Her mode of achieving them was, as might be expected, odd. The disorder of her draperies was made even more noticeable by the fact that they now smelled strongly of the chemicals that she used in her photography. The same smell exhaled from her studio and dark-room, mingling strangely with that of the sweet briar in the garden outside. Photography also gave scope to her instinct for domination. She press-ganged anyone she knew into coming to her studio to have his or her picture taken. She tried to do the same to people she did not know. 'Why does not Miss Smith come to be photographed?' she once asked. 'I hear she is beautiful. Bid her come and she will be made immortal!' The Poet Laureate, the Master of Balliol College, Oxford, a laundry-maid at the wash-tub, a handsome fisherman mending his nets by his boat – each and all found themselves swept, breathless and bewildered, into the chicken-house to pose for their pictures. This was not a light ordeal: often it meant sitting in the same uncomfortable attitude for twenty minutes on end. Mrs Cameron was a perfectionist: if her first attempt failed, she forced her sitter to help her repeat the process till she got the desired result.

Sometimes she wanted to take a straightforward portrait: but she might also require her sitter to act as model in some scene taken from scripture or legend or her own romantic imagination. This was likely to prove an even greater strain than sitting for a portrait. The sitters might be compelled to stay for half an hour clutched in each other's arms to represent Lancelot and Guinevere in a love scene. These 'fancy' pictures of Mrs Cameron's were a great success with the public: so much so that in 1874 she was invited to provide the illustrations for a new edition of Tennyson's *The Idylls of the King*. Excitedly, she looked about for models. She soon discovered an admirable King Arthur in the person of a porter working on the quayside at Yarmouth. But she was hard put to it to find a Sir Lancelot. One evening she and Tennyson attended a party to meet a famous Roman Catholic dignitary, Cardinal Vaughan. 'Alfred,' cried Mrs Cameron joyously, as she caught sight of the Cardinal, 'Alfred, I have found Sir Lancelot!' Tennyson commented dubiously, 'I want a face well worn with human passion.' How far the Cardinal answered to this description is not recorded. But there is no photograph of him in the role of Sir Lancelot.

Mrs Cameron's illustrations to *The Idylls of the King* represented the climax of her association with Tennyson. After this, though their feelings for each other did not alter, their ways drew apart. Inevitably; for in 1875 the Camerons left England to settle in Ceylon where Mr Cameron had a property. It was his decision. He might have been expected to play second fiddle to his powerful wife. In fact he was always the master. She wished him to be, she looked up to him. This was partly on account of his impressive looks. 'Behold the most beautiful old man in the world!' she once exclaimed, throwing open the door to reveal him to a visitor; and she delighted to photograph him. Good-humouredly he submitted to the ordeal but in no very serious spirit. A scene from *The Idylls of the King* was nearly spoiled because taking part in it sent Charles Cameron into fits of laughter, which he made no attempt to control. He took a detached attitude also to his wife's social activities; welcomed her guests courteously, but if more arrived than he found comfortable, he quietly retired to bed until the house was emptier. Nor was there any question that it was he who made the important decisions about the family way of life. He had always loved the East – that was why he retained his Ceylon property. Now at eighty years old he decided he wanted to spend his last days there: all the more so because four of his sons, of whom he was very fond, had made their lives in the East. Mrs Cameron seems to have made no objection to his decision; she too wanted to see her sons.

Accordingly one afternoon in 1875 the port of Southampton saw a large company of distinguished persons assembled at the quayside to say goodbye to the Camerons. They confronted a striking spectacle: Mr Cameron with his white hair falling about his shoulders holding an ivory-handled stick in one hand and in the other a rose presented to him by Tennyson; Mrs Cameron moving animatedly about and pressing some of her photographs on bewildered porters by way of a tip. Behind them were piled innumerable pieces of luggage; to which were added two coffins to be ready in case Mr and Mrs Cameron died on the voyage, and a live cow to ensure that they had fresh milk during the many weeks that must elapse before they reached Ceylon. Once on board, Mrs Cameron spent her time writing letters to be posted to England from every port of call. They maintained a steady level of exalted rapture, notably when she referred to her husband.

> I need not tell you that amidst all this bustling world of 380 people, my husband sits in majesty like a being from another sphere, his white hair shining like the foam of the sea and his white hands holding on each side his golden chain . . . O what good it does to one's soul to go forth! How it heals all the little frets and insect-stings of life, to feel the pulse of the large world and to count all men as one's brethren and to merge one's individual self in the thoughts of the mighty whole!

In 1878 Mrs Cameron came back to England, but only for a short visit. For the rest she spent her later days at her home in the Ceylon hills, surrounded by groves of cocoa and casuarina trees, made lively by the flutterings of exotic birds and the gambols of grey-whiskered monkeys. There she occupied herself with photographing, letter-writing and ecstatically contemplating the beauties of nature. She contrived to remain ecstatic literally to her last breath. In January 1879 she was suddenly taken ill. A few nights later, lying in bed, she looked up through the window at the starlit sky. 'Beautiful!' she sighed rapturously; and died.

II

Mrs Cameron's art reflected her personality: vital, original and adventurous, always romantic, sometimes comic. Like much in the Victorian age, it looked both backward and forward, was both experimental and traditional. In so far as it employed a new medium, it was experimental. But it represented a traditional taste, a traditional artistic ideal. It aimed at beauty as already manifested in painting, more particularly in the painting of her friends, Watts and the Pre-Raphaelites. Like theirs, her work divided itself into two categories: her portraits and her 'fancy' pictures. It is true that for these she was forced to use living models. But so too did Watts and the Pre-Raphaelites. Mary and the Angel in Rossetti's picture of the Annunciation were drawn from his sister Christina and her suitor James Collinson; Millais persuaded Elizabeth Siddal to lie for hours on end fully clothed in a bath of water to serve as a model for the drowning Ophelia. In the same way, Mrs Cameron used her parlour-maid Mary Hillier and a little neighbour called Freddy Gould to act as models for the Madonna and Cupid respectively; on one occasion she kept a young female friend lying on a bare floor for two and a half hours holding a strange man's ankle in order to represent the repentant Guinevere prostrate at the foot of an indignant King Arthur. The young friend's description of this experience conjures up a comic picture. Indeed, though intended so seriously, it is in the *Idylls of the King* illustrations that Mrs Cameron's comic side irresistibly reveals itself. The figures in them are so wonderfully unlike Lancelot and Guinevere and the rest of them, and so wonderfully like what in fact they were: a group of Victorian persons got up to take part in amateur theatricals and showing themselves awkward and self-conscious at the prospect.

None of the pictures in this album is as comic as that. Mary Hillier looks sufficiently Madonna-like, and Freddy Gould makes a pretty Cupid. But there is no question that one is a Victorian girl and the other a Victorian little boy: no more than the figures in the *Idylls* illustrations do they convey a convincing illusion of reality. The truth is that there is an unbridgeable gulf in such pictures between medium and subject. Photographs inevitably suggest a period when or after photography was invented. The photograph of a man dressed in the costume of a pre-photographic age, however accurately, cannot help giving the impression of a man of his own day dressed up. This is not to say that Mrs Cameron's 'fancy' pictures are complete failures. They are often pretty in themselves and they embody the Romantic daydream in terms entertainingly Victorian. This gives them charm: the fact that they make one smile adds to the charm.

In Mrs Cameron's portraits, on the other hand, there is nothing to smile at. For here there is no difficulty in reconciling subject and medium. Whether it be the work of brush or of camera, a portrait is tethered to the facts of here-and-now. It can only depict reality and contemporary reality: fancy has little part to play in it, and the artist's creative faculty shows in his power imaginatively and individually to interpret his model. Holbein's portraits of Henry VIII are both an accurate record of Henry's features and an expression of Holbein's penetrating inter-pretation of his character. So also Mrs Cameron: her photographs are at once likenesses and interpretations. These interpretations are in tune with her vision of reality as a whole. She noted above all those qualities in her sitters which aroused her admiration. In children and young women this was their beauty. Her portraits of her niece Julia Duckworth (later to be the mother of Virginia Woolf) are portraits of her beauty; for to Mrs Cameron, it was this that chiefly distinguished her from other women. This beauty has for us the added interest of being the sort that appealed most to the Victorians; or rather to the serious and idealistic Victorians like Ruskin and George Eliot. This meant a beauty with nothing sensual about it, but grave, noble, aspiring like that of George Eliot's Dorothea Brooke.

Miss Brooke had that kind of beauty which seems to be thrown into relief by poor dress. Her hand and wrist were so finely formed that she could wear sleeves not less bare of style than those in which the Blessed Virgin appeared to Italian painters; and her profile as well as her stature and bearing seemed to gain the more dignity from her plain garments, which by the side of the provincial fashion gave her the impressiveness of a fine quotation from the Bible.

The children in Mrs Cameron's photographs too are never impish or animal but Words-worthian cherubs, wide-eyed and solemn, almost visibly trailing clouds of glory, almost audibly lisping intimations of immortality. Yet neither children nor young women are idealised, in the bad sense of the word. Mrs Cameron made it a principle never to touch up a print. These pictures, while expressing her ideal vision of femininity and of childhood, are also accurate likenesses of their subjects.

The same is true of her portraits of men; and more impressively. For her male subjects are more impressive. She liked photographing men, as she liked photographing women, because she admired them. But whereas she admired women for their looks, she admired men mainly for their souls and minds. Her aim in photographing men was to make these apparent. She had good material to work on. Almost all the great writers and artists of the age sat for her. Some of her best portraits of them are in this album, likenesses of Browning, Watts, Holman Hunt, and of course Tennyson.

Tennyson was doubly qualified to excite her admiration; he was beautiful as well as a literary genius. She did justice to his beauty but still more to his genius; its rich imagination, its passion, its strength. Not however at the expense of his humanity; here is a real flesh and blood man. But he is a man who could write 'Maud' and 'In Memoriam'. Mrs Cameron's is the best likeness of Tennyson that there is, better than Watts' picture in the National Portrait Gallery, better than Rejlander's photograph reproduced in this album. More exactly than either does it keep the balance between body and soul. Watts' brooding bard, haloed by shadowy laurels, is almost disembodied; Rejlander shows us a good-looking Victorian gentleman with no special sign of soul about him. Tennyson appreciated Mrs Cameron's achievement. Though he called her picture 'The Dirty Monk', it was his favourite portrait of himself.

Mrs Cameron's photographs make up half of the album. The rest is composed of portraits by other distinguished artistic photographers of the time, notably Lewis Carroll, of groups of schoolboys and lawyers and house-parties professionally photographed, and of a number of more informal studies of life at Freshwater featuring Mrs Cameron's family and friends and household. The whole adds up to a general picture of that world in which the Pattle sisters were moving spirits. The impression made by it is like that made by Mrs Cameron herself: distinguished, unique and a touch comic. There is no doubt about the distinction; most of the great artists and thinkers of the time had a foot in it. It is unique and comic because it is such a curious mixture of incongruities, of Romantic dreams and Victorian facts. Socially and economically, it was part of the upper-middle and professional classes of the time and representative of it. Since its members were drawn from the more thoughtful of this class, their views tended to be liberal and their manners often unconventional. But this did not mean they were rebellious, let alone lawless. Prosperous, stable, responsible, they believed firmly in the social order to which they were born and accepted its basic values. They were in favour of family life and fidelity in marriage and setting a good example and keeping the law and paying their bills.

Their culture on the other hand derived from the great Romantic poets of the previous generation, and its spirit was enthusiastically romantic, full of sentiment and daydream, scornful of the prudent and the commonplace, ever yearning after some ideal beauty hardly to be found on this humdrum earth. Such a culture did not harmonise ultimately with Victorian orthodox values and mode of living: it was not law-abiding or responsible or domestic, as these words were generally understood in nineteenth-century England. On the contrary, the Romantic spirit, if given its head, was likely to threaten the security of the Victorian social order. Obscurely aware of this, the great men who inspired the Pattle circle had tried to effect a compromise, sought to tame the Romantic spirit and, while maintaining its fervour, to divert it into the service of respectable Victorian objectives. Tennyson celebrated romantic love but identified it with married love. Watts preached the sacredness of art as a necessary part of the Good Life: but his notion of the Good Life was one that could be approved of by a Victorian citizen and family man.

They and their supporters put forward this compromise view with energy and eloquence. But the fact remained that it was a compromise and an uneasy one. The Romantic spirit was not to be tamed even by the most eminent of Victorians. Shelley, the family man, is an unconvincing figure; Wordsworth would have felt uncomfortable at a Freshwater picnic; Lancelot and Guinevere looked out of place at Dimbola. They even looked comic. And not Lancelot and Guinevere only; incongruity is mirth-provoking. It is impossible to look at the Pattle world as depicted in this album without now and again smiling.

Yet it should not be a superior smile. We, in the 1970s, are in no position to look down on Mrs Cameron and her friends. The superiority is on their side: their achievements prove it. What poet have we equal to Tennyson or Browning? What portraitist as good as Mrs Cameron? And the social life illustrated in these pages is surely both more agreeable and more stimulating than anything comparable today. I doubt if there is now any place where poets and painters can find the inspiration – let alone the fun – that Tennyson and Watts found at Freshwater. Looking through this album I may sometimes smile: but more often I feel envious.

Preface

by GRAHAM OVENDEN

I

MIA (MARIA) JACKSON was one of the three beauties among the Pattle sisters, and her descendants perhaps the most notable. Her grandchildren included William Wyamar Vaughan, Headmaster of Rugby, H. A. L. Fisher, famous for the Education Act of 1918, Adeline Fisher, wife of Ralph Vaughan Williams, Edmund Fisher, the architect, Sir William Fisher, Admiral of the Fleet, Gerald Duckworth, the publisher, Vanessa Bell, the painter, and Virginia Woolf, the writer.

In 1863 Julia Margaret Cameron gave her sister Mia a photograph album. It was bound in green leather and on the front were mounted the letters MIA in brass.

This album, containing works both by Julia Margaret Cameron and by other photographers, is probably one of the most interesting documents to come from Mrs Cameron's hands. Whereas the majority of her presentation albums are to be considered primarily as a complete unit, a work of art, the Mia album is first and foremost a family album. This is not to detract from its aesthetic, for it contains much which is fine, but more to enhance it since its view into the remarkable circle of Pattledom is of such interest.

First, there is Mrs Cameron's contribution of her own images that relate intimately to the family, sons, nieces, brothers-in-law, husband. There are many photographs of Julia Duckworth, Mia's youngest daughter (who was, with Mary Hillier, surely the most photographed of Mrs Cameron's models). Also represented are Mrs Cameron's idols, Tennyson, Taylor, de Vere, Browning, Watts, Holman Hunt, as are the chance Freshwater neighbours such as the Koewen sisters and Freddy Gould.

The pictures of Mrs Cameron, her family and servants are of particular value, evoking the life and atmosphere around Dimbola, the Camerons' house at Freshwater. The bustle and presence of Mrs Cameron come much closer to us. We see the well where, with nitrate-stained fingers, she carried out her labour of artistic love: 'For in all freezing weather I have poured nine cans of water fresh from the well over each photograph.' It is revealing to see Mary Hillier as maid and not just as the Madonna of Mrs Cameron's compositions, to see Mary Ryan's real beauty.

In personal content the Mia album is very typical of volumes from the Victorian era. It only lacks the image of the great queen and her consort (perhaps the photograph of 'Bertie' and his mentors – Pl. 32 – makes up for this) to make it a complete reflection of the nineteenth-century attitude in making up an album of this type. What makes it different from the countless products of many Victorian families is that here are presented the documents not only of existence but also of art. How, with the Pattle obsession for beauty, could it be otherwise?

It is obvious from Mrs Cameron's presentation albums – and the Mia album is no exception in this respect – that she considered the allegory to have equal expressive importance as her works of straight portraiture. Though a number of her more complex images are badly constructed and sentimentalised to an unpalatable pitch, it is unjust and incorrect to dismiss categorically her romantic vision as inferior to the dignified rendering of the Victorian intelligentsia which has been acclaimed as her forte. There are many photographs which border between the allegory and the portrait, for example 'The Dream' (Pl. 23), which possess a Pre-Raphaelite melancholy while preserving the simplicity of manner of her straight portraiture.

It is always interesting and revealing to see an artist's choice of his own work. In the Mia album we see not only Mrs Cameron's own contribution but also her choice of the work of her friends and contemporaries. Whether it be a reproduction of a painting by G. F. Watts or a Rejlander photographic composition, this is a rich selection indeed.

II

The album was made up of two sections, the front for Mrs Cameron's work, and the back – the album being inverted and reversed – for non-Cameron material (with five possible exceptions). All the images were taken by the wet collodion (plate) process and the positive prints were made on gold-toned albumenised paper.

In order to achieve the highest quality of reproduction in this edition of the album, the 119 plates have been rearranged by density of image. Their original sequence is indicated by the second number by each caption.

A number of the photographs bear on the reverse Mrs Cameron's precise directions as to their positioning in the original album. This is somewhat puzzling, for the non-Cameron material in particular bears a considerable air of the haphazard, although the directions were properly followed. In addition, Mrs Cameron's pursuit of the photographic art did not reach full sway until the end of 1863, and much of her material could not have been ready for presentation on 7th July 1863, the date inscribed in the album. These facts suggest possibly that the album, when presented, was largely incomplete, much of the material being added later.

Three photographers were responsible for many of the photographs among the non-Cameron material: Charles Dodgson or Lewis Carroll is famous of course as author of the Alice books, but recently however he has become equally famous (at least to the photographic enthusiast) as one of the giants of Victorian amateur photography. His photographs of children must be considered of the first importance and among the finest of nineteenth-century portraiture.

Oscar Gustave Rejlander (1813–75) started his career as a portrait-painter in Rome where his work also included the copying of Old Masters. In 1852 he moved to England, settling in Lincoln. His first intimate contact with photography (as with so many other Victorian photographers) came when he took up the idea of using the photographic image as an aid to painting portraits. He took lessons in photographic technique in 1853 and opened a studio in Wolverhampton in 1855. Though he is best known as the perpetrator of such high art photography as 'The Two Ways of Life' (1857), an allegorical photomontage much in the manner of H. P. Robinson, it is his evocative portraits of children and genre subjects which are his chief contribution to the advancement of nineteenth-century photography. His work was admired by both Julia Margaret Cameron and Lewis Carroll, to whom he gave assistance at their request.

Lord Somers – Charles Somers-Cocks, Viscount Eastnor, 3rd Earl Somers – was married to Virginia Pattle, one of Mrs Cameron's sisters. In his youth he had wished to become a painter. His mother's speedy rebuff had been 'as a member of the aristocracy you can only paint badly'. Fortunately he directed his artistic bent towards photography, eventually becoming Vice-President of the Photographic Society of London. There was considerable sympathy between Lord Somers and his sister-in-law Mrs Cameron, and he helped her stage a number of exhibitions. Perhaps it should be added that not only was he a patron of the arts (particularly of Edward Lear) but also a Member of Parliament for six years and a Lord in Waiting to Queen Victoria.

It is still unknown whether it was Somers or Rejlander who took the Dimbola photographs. I have found as yet no concrete evidence in the thirteen albums relating to the Pattle circle which I have seen. However, I believe, after exhaustive research, that the majority are by Rejlander, although, needless to say, there will always be a degree of conjecture until contemporary inscribed material comes to light.

III

I must record my acknowledgments to those who have helped and advised me: Russ Anderson, Esq, Mrs John Bennett, Mrs Norman Butler, Miss Elizabeth French Boyd, Commander A. E. H. Cameron, Sir Weldon Dalrymple-Champneys, Bt, C.B., Colin Ford, Esq, Professor Margaret Harker, The Hon. Mrs B. A. F. Hervey-Bathurst, Sir Gyles Isham, Bt, Miss Virginia Isham, Mrs Charles Norman, Mrs V. Packe, Roger T. Pattle, Esq, Dame Janet Vaughan, Sir Charles Tennyson.

THE PLATES

KEY TO CAPTIONS

The first number indicates the sequence of this volume.

The second (italic) number refers to the sequence of the original album.

The first name is that of the photographer (or artist).

The second name is that of the sitter or subject. Titles in italic are the photographers' own.

1 *(25)* J. M. Cameron

Unknown sitter

c. 1865–6

187 by 150 mm/7.4 by 5.9 in

2 *(18)*   J. M. Cameron

Mrs Herbert Fisher?

c. 1865–6

224 by 185 mm/8.8 by 7.3 in

MARY JACKSON, the second daughter of Maria and John Jackson, married Herbert
Fisher and bore him eleven children.

3 (38)   J. M. Cameron

James Spedding

Hendon Lawn, Whitsuntide 1864

218 by 175 mm/8.6 by 6.9 in

SPEDDING was a friend of Tennyson and the biographer of Francis Bacon.

James Spedding

4 *(17)*   J. M. Cameron

Mrs Herbert Duckworth

c. 1866

237 by 190 mm/9.4 by 7.5 in

JULIA JACKSON was the youngest daughter of Maria and Dr John Jackson. Her first husband was Herbert Duckworth, a barrister. Of her three children by this marriage, Sir George Duckworth became Secretary to the Royal Commission on Historical Monuments, and Gerald l'Étang Duckworth founded in 1898 the publishing firm which bears his name.

In 1870 Julia was left a widow. She married her second husband, Leslie Stephen, eight years later. He was a literary journalist, biographer, and editor of the Dictionary of National Biography. Her four children by this marriage included Vanessa (Bell), the painter, and Virginia (Woolf), the writer.

Julia was one of the most photographed of Mrs Cameron's models. Her beauty was also recorded by Virginia Woolf in her novel *To The Lighthouse*. Of Mrs Ramsay (Julia) she writes: 'The Graces assembling seemed to have joined hands in meadows of Asphodel to compose that face.'

5 *(95)* Unknown photographer, possibly Jabez Hughes or O. G. Rejlander

Sir Henry Taylor

c. 1863–5

100 by 64 mm/3.9 by 2.5 in

THOUGH an official of eminence at the Colonial Office, Henry Taylor (1800–86) refused elevation to the post of Under-Secretary: he preferred the pursuit of poetry. His major work in the vein was *Philip Van Artevelde*, first published in 1834. Though this verse drama had an immediate popular success, it was viewed by many of the Victorian literary world with indifference. It is of little importance today. Macready staged it in 1847 and it failed after only six performances.

However, Mrs Cameron considered Taylor's genius of the highest order and they were long and intimate friends: she described him as 'the friend of thirty-eight years and the Godfather of my child'. She invited him to Dimbola every spring and autumn and he appears more often than any other male sitter in her photographs.

6 *(5)*   J. M. Cameron

Mrs Herbert Duckworth

c. 1865–6

238 by 191 mm/9.4 by 7.5 in

7 (7)   J. M. Cameron

Mrs Herbert Duckworth

c. 1865–6

218 by 168 mm/8.6 by 6.6 in

8 *(31)* J. M. Cameron

Paul and Virginia (cf. Pl. 10)

1865

248 by 208 mm/9.8 by 8.2 in

FREDDY GOULD and Lizzie Koewen.
 The Koewen sisters appear in a number of Mrs Cameron's allegorical compositions. They were the daughters of the commander of the forts on the Isle of Wight.

9 *(34)*   J. M. Cameron

Sir Henry Taylor

Freshwater, 1864

243 by 183 mm/9.6 by 7.2 in

10 *(32)*   J. M. Cameron

Paul and Virginia

1865

252 by 206 mm/9.9 by 8.1 in

FREDDY GOULD and Lizzie Koewen.

11 *(40)*   J. M. Cameron

Henry Herschel Hay Cameron

c. 1865

242 by 200 mm/9.5 by 7.9 in

HENRY was the youngest son of Julia and Charles Hay Cameron. He followed his mother's interest in photography, and became an accomplished portrait photographer.

12 *(28)*   J. M. Cameron

Madonna and Child

Freshwater, 1865

250 by 199 mm/9.9 by 7.9 in

MARY HILLIER and Freddy Gould.

13 *(51)*   J. M. Cameron

The Guardian Angel

September, 1868

288 by 155 mm/11.3 by 6.1 in

STUDY of Hattie Campbell.

14 *(48)*   J. M. Cameron

Our beautiful "Birdie"

November, 1869

305 by 230 mm/12.0 by 9.1 in

ANNIE CHINERY, who married Ewen Cameron, the second son of Julia and Charles Hay Cameron, was the daughter of Edward Chinery, M.D.

our beautiful "Birdie"

15 *(56)* J. M. Cameron

G. F. Watts

Taken on Cromwell Place balcony, 1864

215 mm/8.5 in circle

GEORGE FREDERIC WATTS (1817–1904) was the son of an impoverished piano-maker and tuner. He showed considerable promise as a painter in his youth, and by the time he was sixteen he was able to earn a living by painting portraits. He was accepted by the Royal Academy Schools, and in 1842 won a prize of £300 for his cartoon of Caractacus for the new decorative scheme at Westminster Palace.

Watts lived for nearly thirty years with Mrs Cameron's sister and brother-in-law, Sarah and Thoby Prinsep, at Little Holland House, Kensington, and at The Briary, I.O.W. He painted many of the Pattle sisters and their children, including Julia Margaret (see Pls 59, 64, 73, 94).

Watts married Ellen Terry in 1864. It was an unfortunate attachment and they soon parted, though their estrangement was not made public until 1877. This is one of the few occasions when the Pattle sisters appear in a thoroughly bad light: for once Julia Cameron's unrealistic romanticism and Sarah Prinsep's meddling caused real harm.

Watts was Mrs Cameron's artistic mentor and had considerable influence over her allegorical compositions, though not always for the best.

G. F. Watts

16 *(9)* J. M. Cameron

H. Thoby Prinsep

c. 1869

252 by 203 mm/9.9 by 8.0 in

PRINSEP held numerous administrative posts in Calcutta, as well as the appointment of Persian Secretary to the Government, and subsequently a seat on the Council of India. He married Sarah Pattle, Mrs Cameron's sister, in 1835. It was on their removal to Little Holland House in Kensington that the famous salon – Sarah's contribution to Pattledom – came into being, offering Mrs Cameron a cache of 'beauty and intellect' to sit before her camera.

17 *(43)*   J. M. Cameron

Divine Love

c. 1865

240 by 183 mm/9.5 by 7.2 in

MARY HILLIER and Freddy Gould.

18 *(15)*   J. M. Cameron

The Dirty Monk

1865

247 by 200 mm/9.7 by 7.9 in

ALFRED TENNYSON (1809–92) was the idol of his age, being appointed Poet Laureate in 1850 in succession to Wordsworth. His popularity remained immense until his death. His influence fell not only on his fellow poets, but encompassed the visual arts as well, in particular the Pre-Raphaelites.

In 1853 the Tennysons bought Farringford, an estate at Freshwater on the Isle of Wight. Seven years later the Camerons, who had been friends with the Tennysons for some years, became their neighbours. This was an ideal arrangement for Julia Margaret Cameron, for the noble and illustrious who visited Tennyson were at hand to be wooed before her camera. Tennyson was seduced on many occasions to sit for Mrs Cameron, although this entailed a degree of protest and grumbling from the Laureate: witness William Allingham's anecdote.

Allingham to Tennyson: '. . . They ought to let you go free as a poet.'

Tennyson: 'They charge me double! And I can't go anonymous,' turning to Mrs Cameron, 'by reason of your confounded photographs.'

'The Dirty Monk' was, with Mayall's severe studio photograph, Tennyson's favourite image of himself. It was probably the Laureate's (at times) Rabelaisian sense of humour that prompted him to christen this image thus. Mrs Cameron used 'The Dirty Monk' as the frontispiece to Volume One of the 1874 edition of *The Idylls of the King*, a two-volume work published at Tennyson's wish and containing twenty-four photographic illustrations by Mrs Cameron.

19 *(46)*   J. M. Cameron

My Ewens Bride of the 18th November, 1869

November, 1869

309 by 220 mm/12.2 by 8.7 in

ANNIE CHINERY.

My Owens Bride of the 18th November 1869.

20 *(30)*   J. M. Cameron

Yes or No

c. 1865

249 by 200 mm/9.8 by 7.9 in

UNKNOWN model left, Mary Hillier right.

21 *(47)*   J. M. Cameron

Annie Chinery

1869

304 by 229 mm/12.0 by 9.0 in

22 *(44)*   J. M. Cameron

The Kiss of Peace

1869

324 by 242 mm/12.8 by 9.5 in

FLORENCE ANSON? and Mary Hillier.

The Kiss of Peace

23 *(50)* J. M. Cameron

The Dream

April, 1869

289 by 225 mm/11.4 by 8.9 in

PROFILE study of Mary Hillier. Mrs Cameron considered this photograph her second most successful attempt at the art.

24 *(I I)*   J. M. Cameron

Daisy

1864

190 by 146 mm/7.5 by 5.8 in

PROBABLY Margaret, the daughter of Granville Bradley, Dean of Westminster.

25 *(64)*   O. G. Rejlander

Alfred Tennyson

c. 1863

195 by 142 mm/7.7 by 5.6 in

26 *(26)*   J. M. Cameron

Trimmed detail from *Summer Days* (Pl. 86)

c. 1866

144 by 197 mm/5.6 by 7.8 in

FREDDY GOULD and Lizzie Koewen.

27 *(90)*   Unknown photographer

William Bayley

c. 1862–5

96 by 66 mm/3.8 by 2.6 in

BAYLEY was the son of Louisa Pattle and H. V. Bayley.

28 *(23)*   J. M. Cameron

Mrs Herbert Duckworth

c. 1866

237 by 190 mm/9.4 by 7.5 in

ONE wonders whether Mrs Cameron may have had the pre-photographic silhouette in mind, when she scraped the background black in this profile portrait of Mrs Duckworth. The effect is certainly unfortunate, as in all cases when Mrs Cameron tampered with the photographic emulsion.

29 *(73)*   O. G. Rejlander

At the Well

1864

175 by 145 mm/6.9 by 5.7 in

TAKEN at Dimbola, Freshwater. The group includes Hardinge Hay Cameron and the Alderson sisters.

30 *(118)*   W. Jeffrey

Portrait bust of Alfred Tennyson, by Thomas Woolner

202 by 135 mm/8.0 by 5.4 in

WOOLNER (1825–92) was a founder member of the Pre-Raphaelite Brotherhood. This bust now stands in Westminster Abbey.

31 *(83)*　Lewis Carroll

Harry Cameron

1859

100 by 128 mm/3.9 by 5.1 in

HARRY was a nephew of Charles Hay Cameron.

32 *(58)*   Published by Hills and Saunders
(photographer unknown)

General Bruce, Herbert Fisher,
Edward, Prince of Wales, Colonel Kebbel?
(from left to right)

Oxford, 1858

196 by 230 mm/7.8 by 9.1 in

HERBERT FISHER married Mary, the second daughter of Maria and John Jackson. He
was a brilliant barrister and was recommended as guide and mentor to Albert Edward,
Prince of Wales.

33 *(10)* J. M. Cameron

Unknown sitter

c. 1865–8

233 by 199 mm/9.2 by 7.9 in

34 *(119)* Unknown photographer

The High Court of Judicature, Calcutta, 1866–7

139 by 222 mm/5.5 by 8.8 in

Sitting figures, from the left:
1 Mr Justice Trevor   2 Mr Justice [H.V.] Bayley
3 Mr Justice Seton-Karr   4 The Chief Justice
   Sir Barnes Peacock   5 Mr Justice Morgan
6 Mr Justice Loch
Standing figures, from the left:
1 Mr Justice Macpherson   2 Mr Justice Glover
3 Mr Justice Elp [?] Jackson   4 Mr Justice Phear
5 Mr Justice Steer   6 Mr Justice [Baboo] Shumboonath Pundit
7 Mr Justice Kemp   8 Mr Justice Campbell   9 Mr Justice Norman

Key to the Group –

Sitting figures – From the Left.

1 Mr. Justice Trevor – 2 Mr. Justice Bayley
3 Mr. Justice Setun Kan. 4 The Chief Justice
   Sir Barnes Peacock – 5 Mr. Justice Morgan
6 Mr. Justice Loch –

Standing figures – From the left

1. Mr. Justice Macpherson. 2 – Mr. Justice Glover
3 Mr. Justice Elph: Jackson. 4 Mr. Justice Phear
5. Mr. Justice Steer – 6 Mr. Justice Shumbhoonath Pundit
7 Mr. Justice Kemp – 8 Mr. Justice Campbell – 9 Mr. Justice
                                                    Norman

35 *(115)*   A. Moro

Queen Mary Tudor

Photographic reproduction of a painting

261 by 200 mm/10.3 by 7.9 in

A. MORO

MORO. _175._ Portrait de la reine Marie d'Angleterre. (au Musée du Prado)

36 *(1)*   J. M. Cameron

Mrs Herbert Duckworth

c. 1866

245 by 205 mm/9.7 by 8.1 in

37 *(45)*   J. M. Cameron

Annie Chinery

1869

295 by 236 mm / 11.6 by 9.3 in

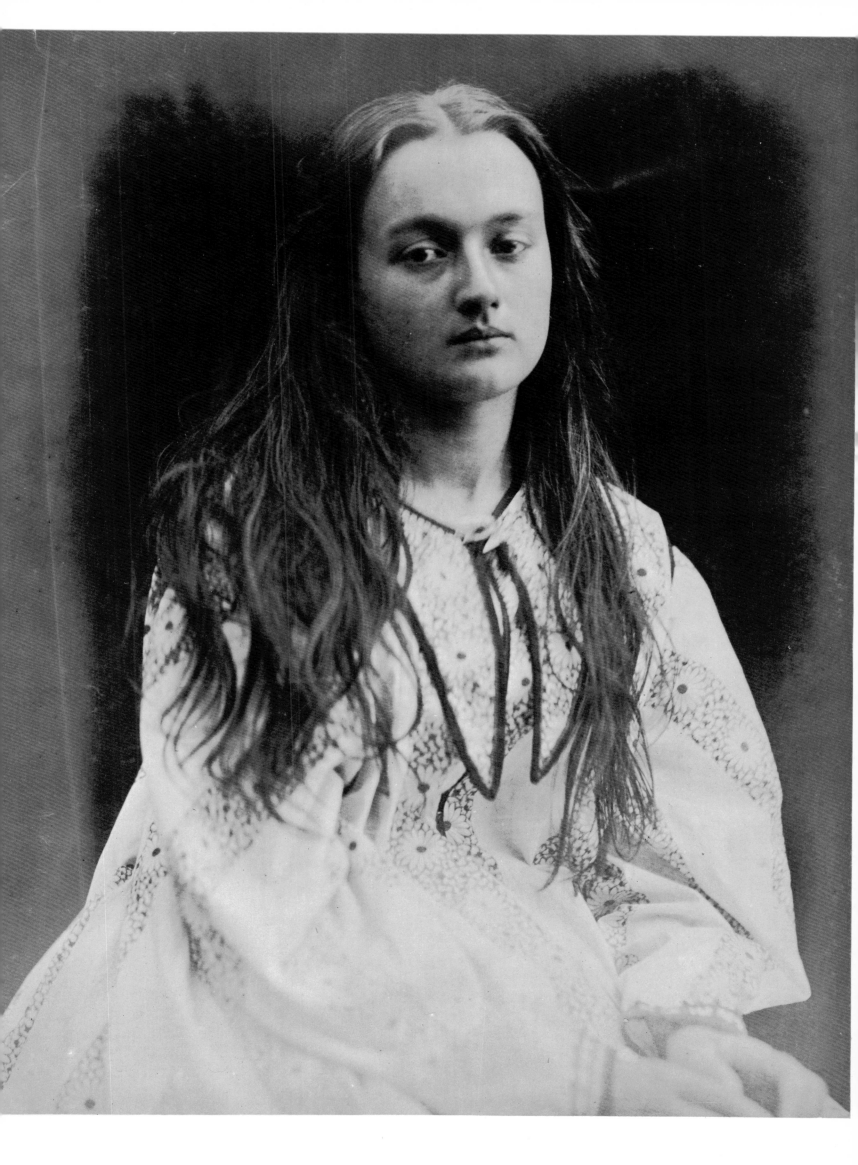

38 *(114)*   Unknown photographer

Anonymous family group

c. 1860–3

97 by 163 mm/3.8 by 6.5 in

39 *(101)* J. M. Cameron

Allegorical group

c. 1868

302 by 258 mm/11.9 by 10.2 in

THE models include May Prinsep (niece of Thoby Prinsep).

40 *(6)*   J. M. Cameron

Mrs Herbert Duckworth

c. 1866

252 by 200 mm/9.9 by 7.9 in

41 *(53)*   J. M. Cameron

Robert Browning

Little Holland House, 1865

198 by 215 mm/7.8 by 8.5 in

JULIA CAMERON was fortunate to obtain a sitting from Browning. As one of the two undisputed giants of Victorian poetry, Browning was an honoured guest with his wife Elizabeth at Little Holland House, the home of Sarah Prinsep. He was one of the many victims of Mrs Cameron's impetuosity. Draped and swathed in blankets, he was left thus posed. It was quite in order that Mrs Cameron's vigorous pursuits should lead to forgetfulness, and Browning sat on, waiting for the advent of the photographer. At last she returned, totally indifferent to poor Browning's lengthy ordeal. This is the least successful of the plates Mrs Cameron took of him.

R. Browning

42 *(4)*   J. M. Cameron

The Sphinx Madonna

Freshwater, 1864

238 by 188 mm/9.4 by 7.4 in

MARY HILLIER and Alice Koewen.

43 *(39)* J. M. Cameron

William Holman Hunt

Hendon Lawn, 1864

223 by 189 mm/8.8 by 7.5 in

HOLMAN HUNT (1827–1910), a founder member of the Pre-Raphaelite Brotherhood, remained the only true practitioner of its original dogmas throughout his painting career. After early struggles his work became much admired by the younger generation of the Victorian art-loving public, and was much reproduced in engravings.

It was Wynfield's photographic portraits of academicians, etc. (including Holman Hunt) that were a great influence on Mrs Cameron's art. It seems appropriate that Mrs Cameron should pose Holman Hunt in Levantine garb, for his dauntless painting expeditions to Egypt were well known to the Little Holland House group.

W. Holman Hunt

44 *(14)*   J. M. Cameron

Charles Hay Cameron

c. 1865

176 by 140 mm/7.0 by 5.5 in

CHARLES HAY CAMERON (1795–1880) was the husband of Julia Margaret Pattle. He was a scholar of great learning and humanity, a Benthamite jurist and philosopher who served as Chairman of the India Law Commission and gave Ceylon its code of legal procedure.

He was twenty years older than his wife, and appears to have been something of a hypochondriac. He always wore magnificent dressing-gowns: his oriental splendour could be seen in and around Dimbola when they settled on the Isle of Wight. It was his impulse that sent the Camerons to Ceylon in 1875, thus greatly curtailing Mrs Cameron's pursuit of the photographic art.

Charles Hay Cameron.

45 *(98)*   Unknown photographer

Portrait of a girl (*cf*. Pl. 79)

c. 1863

136 by 95 mm/5.4 by 3.7 in

46 *(8)*   J. M. Cameron

Aubrey de Vere

c. 1865

240 by 189 mm/9.5 by 7.5 in

DE VERE (1814–1902) was a poet and author of considerable standing. It was at Tennyson's home, Farringford, that Mrs Cameron was introduced to de Vere.

Edmund Gosse wrote of de Vere: 'His countenance bore a singular resemblance to the portraits of Wordsworth although the type was softer and less vigorous. His forehead, which sloped a little and was very high and domed, was much observed in the open air from a trick he had of tilting his tall hat back. I used to think very profanely, that in profile on these occasions he bore a quite absurdly close resemblance to the Hatter in *Alice's Adventures* especially when, as was frequently the case, he recited poetry.'

Aubrey de Vere

47 *(2)*   J. M. Cameron

Mrs Herbert Fisher with, possibly, her eldest son, Herbert A. L.

c. 1865–6

240 by 192 mm/9.5 by 7.6 in

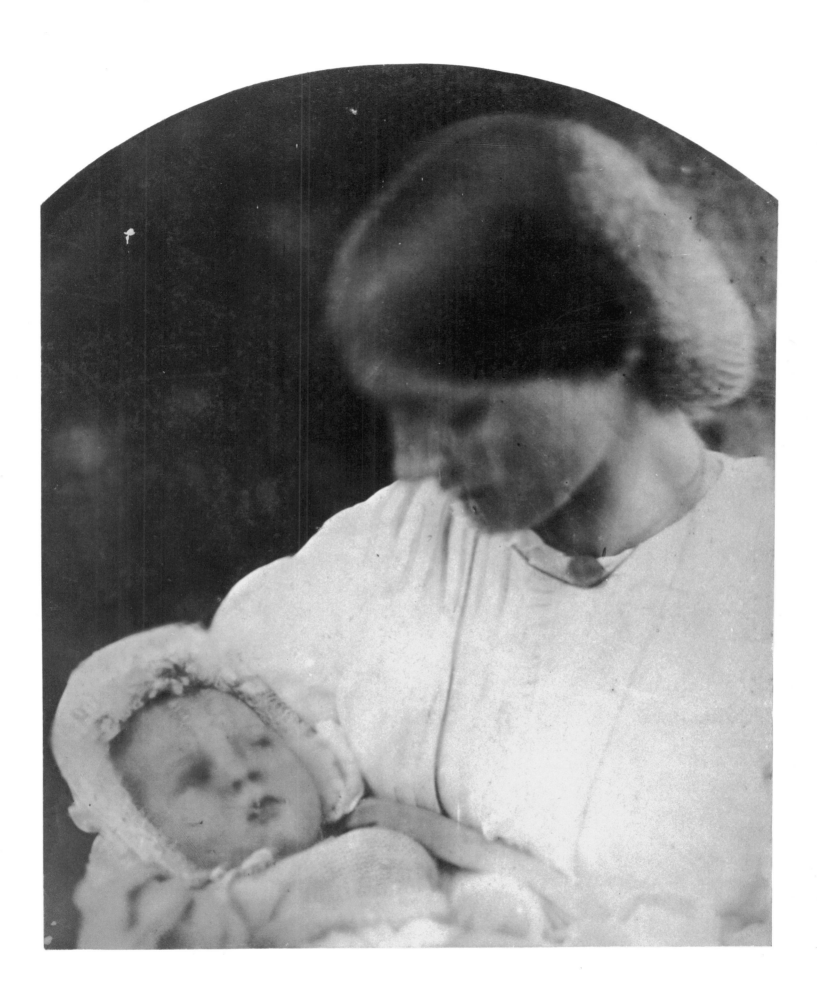

48 *(77)*   Lord Somers (attributed)

Mrs Cameron and maids receive letters
from the postman, Freshwater

c. 1863–5

163 by 113 mm/6.5 by 4.5 in

49 *(99)*   Lord Somers and
O. G. Rejlander?

The hurdy-gurdy man (cf. Pl. 68)

c. 1863–5

115 by 142 mm/4.5 by 5.6 in

THE group includes, possibly, O. G. Rejlander.

50 *(79)*   Lord Somers (attributed)

Mrs Cameron and her staff receiving letters from the postman

c. 1863–5

157 by 116 mm/6.2 by 4.6 in

51 *(113)*   Unknown photographer

Unknown sitter

c. 1860–5

116 by 94 mm/4.6 by 3.7 in

52 *(61)*   Unknown artist

Mrs James Pattle

Reproduction of a painting, *c.* 1815–20

136 by 106 mm/5.4 by 4.2 in

ADELINE PATTLE (1793–1845) was the mother of Julia Margaret Cameron and the daughter of the Chevalier de l'Étang, officer in Louis XVI's Gard du Corps, and Superintendent of the Royal Stud Farm.

53 *(27)*   J. M. Cameron

Mrs Herbert Duckworth

c. 1866

238 by 190 mm/9.4 by 7.5 in

54 *(93)*   Lord Somers (attributed)

A maid at Freshwater

c. 1863–5

151 by 112 mm/6.0 by 4.4 in

55 *(109)*   J. M. Cameron

Henry Halford Vaughan? *(carte-de-visite)*

c. 1868

89 by 58 mm/3.5 by 2.3 in

HENRY HALFORD VAUGHAN (1811–85) married Mrs Cameron's niece, Adeline Jackson. He was Regius Professor of Modern History at Oxford.

56 *(76)*   J. M. Cameron?

Charles Hay Cameron

c. 1864–5

155 by 110 mm/6.1 by 4.3 in

57 *(75)*   O. G. Rejlander or Lord Somers

Mrs Cameron receives a salute from
Henry Herschel Hay Cameron, Freshwater

c. 1863–5

153 by 115 mm/6.0 by 4.5 in

60 *(72)* Lord Somers (attributed)

My Cameron Clan

c. 1863–5

142 by 105 mm/5.6 by 4.1 in

CHARLES, Ewen, Hardinge and Henry Hay Cameron (left to right), four of the five sons of Julia and Charles Hay Cameron. Ewen was later to marry Annie Chinery.

61 *(3)*   J. M. Cameron

Mrs Herbert Duckworth

c. 1865–6

223 by 192 mm/8.8 by 7.6 in

62 *(67)*   Lord Somers (attributed)

Julia Margaret Cameron

c. 1862–5

142 by 103 mm/5.6 by 4.1 in

63 *(96)*   Unknown artist

Possibly Henry Taylor in his youth

Reproduction of a painting

106 by 88 mm/4.2 by 3.5 in

64 *(62)*   G. F. Watts

Julia Margaret Cameron

Reproduction of a study for her portrait, 1852

207 by 172 mm/8.1 by 6.8 in

65 *(78)*   Lord Somers (attributed)

The butcher's visit

c. 1863–5

160 by 112 mm/6.3 by 4.4 in

66 *(85)*   O. G. Rejlander (attributed)

Unknown child

c. 1863–5

115 by 89 mm/4.5 by 3.5 in

67 *(107)*   J. M. Cameron

Charles Hay Cameron *(carte-de-visite)*

c. 1866

86 by 57 mm/3.4 by 2.2 in

CHARLES was the fourth son of Julia and Charles Hay Cameron.

68 *(100)* Lord Somers and
O. G. Rejlander?

The hurdy-gurdy man (cf. Pl. 49)

c. 1863–5

100 by 158 mm/3.9 by 6.3 in

THE group includes, possibly, O. G. Rejlander.

69 *(84)*   Lord Somers (attributed)

Mr and Mrs Henry Halford Vaughan?

c. 1863–5

98 by 69 mm/3.9 by 2.7 in

70 *(66)*   Lord Somers (attributed)

Charles and Henry Cameron

c. 1863–5

135 by 107 mm/5.4 by 4.2 in

71 *(42)*   J. M. Cameron

W. M. Rossetti (wrongly identified as J. A. Froude)

c. 1865

250 by 198 mm/9.9 by 7.8 in

WILLIAM MICHAEL ROSSETTI, brother of the Pre-Raphaelite painter and poet Dante Gabriel Rossetti, was a founder member of the Pre-Raphaelite Brotherhood and editor of its organ *The Germ.*

J. A. Froude

72 *(59)*   J. M. Cameron

Unknown child

c. 1863–4

166 by 116 mm/6.6 by 4.6 in

73 (*106*)   G. F. Watts?

Virginia, Countess Somers

Reproduction of a painting

128 by 112 mm/5.1 by 4.4 in

VIRGINIA PATTLE was a sister of Julia Margaret Cameron. She married Viscount Eastnor, who became Earl Somers.

74 *(29)*   J. M. Cameron

Mrs Herbert Duckworth

c. 1865–6

232 by 176 mm/9.2 by 7.0 in

75 *(116)*   J. E. Millais

Isabella

Reproduction of a painting, 1849

111 by 117 mm/4.4 by 4.6 in

THE models for this painting include William Bell Scott and the Rossetti brothers.

76 *(71)*   O. G. Rejlander or Lewis Carroll

Isabel Somers-Cocks

c. 1860–3

184 by 145 mm/7.3 by 5.7 in

ISABEL was the eldest daughter of Lord and Lady Somers and a niece of Mrs Cameron. She later married Lord Henry Somerset.

77 *(82)*　G. F. Watts

James Spedding

Reproduction of a drawing

188 by 125 mm/7.4 by 4.9 in

78 *(117)* Unknown artist

Oliver Cromwell

Reproduction of a painting

143 by 115 mm/5.6 by 4.5 in

79 *(97)* Lord Somers and O. G. Rejlander?

The Three Graces

c. 1863–5

110 by 160 mm/4.3 by 6.3 in

THE group includes the model who appears in Pl. 45.

80 *(49)*   J. M. Cameron

Ewen's Betrothed

1869

303 by 225 mm/11.9 by 8.9 in

ANNIE CHINERY.

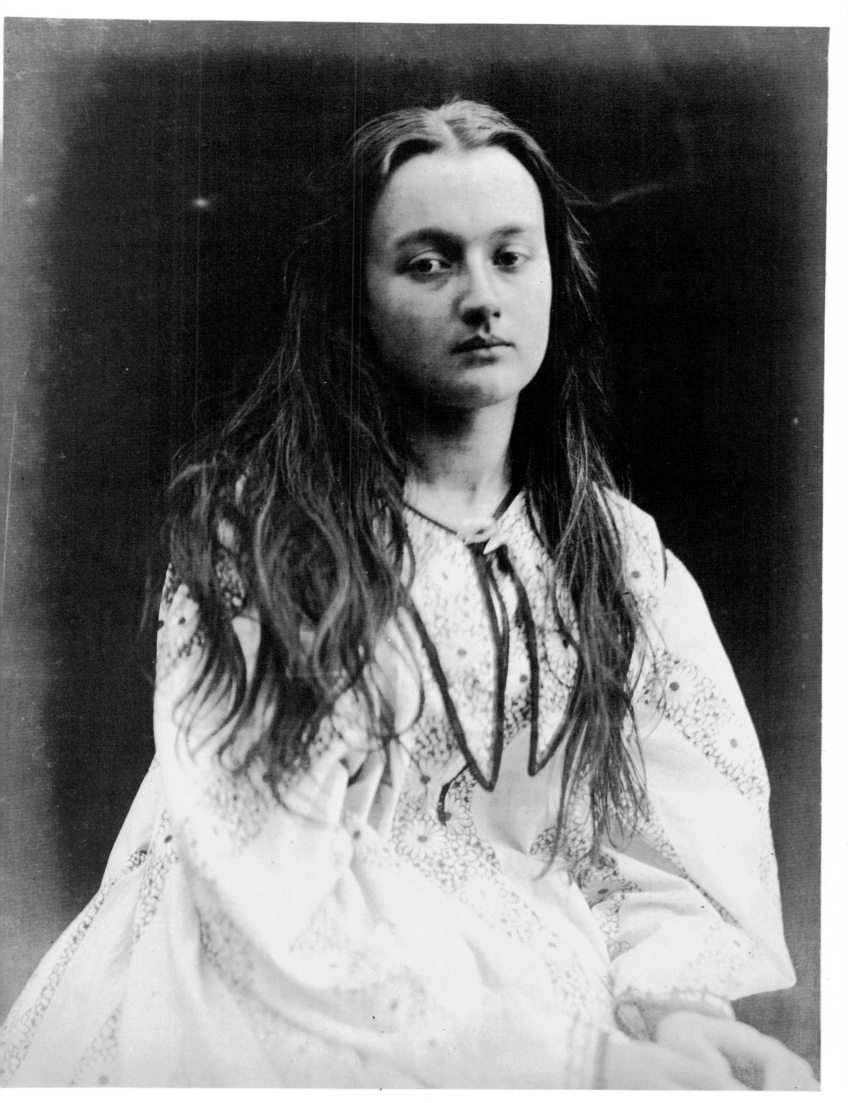

Sven's Betrothed

81 *(19)*   J. M. Cameron

Mrs Herbert Duckworth

c. 1865–6

238 by 203 mm/9.4 by 8.0 in

82 *(54)*   J. M. Cameron

The Echo

c. 1868

278 by 218 mm/11.0 by 8.6 in

THE model is Hattie Campbell.

83 *(57)*   J. M. Cameron

H. Thoby Prinsep

1865

328 by 239 mm / 13.0 by 9.4 in

H. T. Prinsep

84 *(20)*   J. M. Cameron

Mrs Herbert Duckworth

c. 1866

230 by 190 mm/9.1 by 7.5 in

AN experimental plate by Mrs Cameron, fortunately not often repeated.

85 *(36)*   J. M. Cameron

Cupid

1866

282 by 230 mm/11.1 by 9.1 in

FREDDY GOULD.

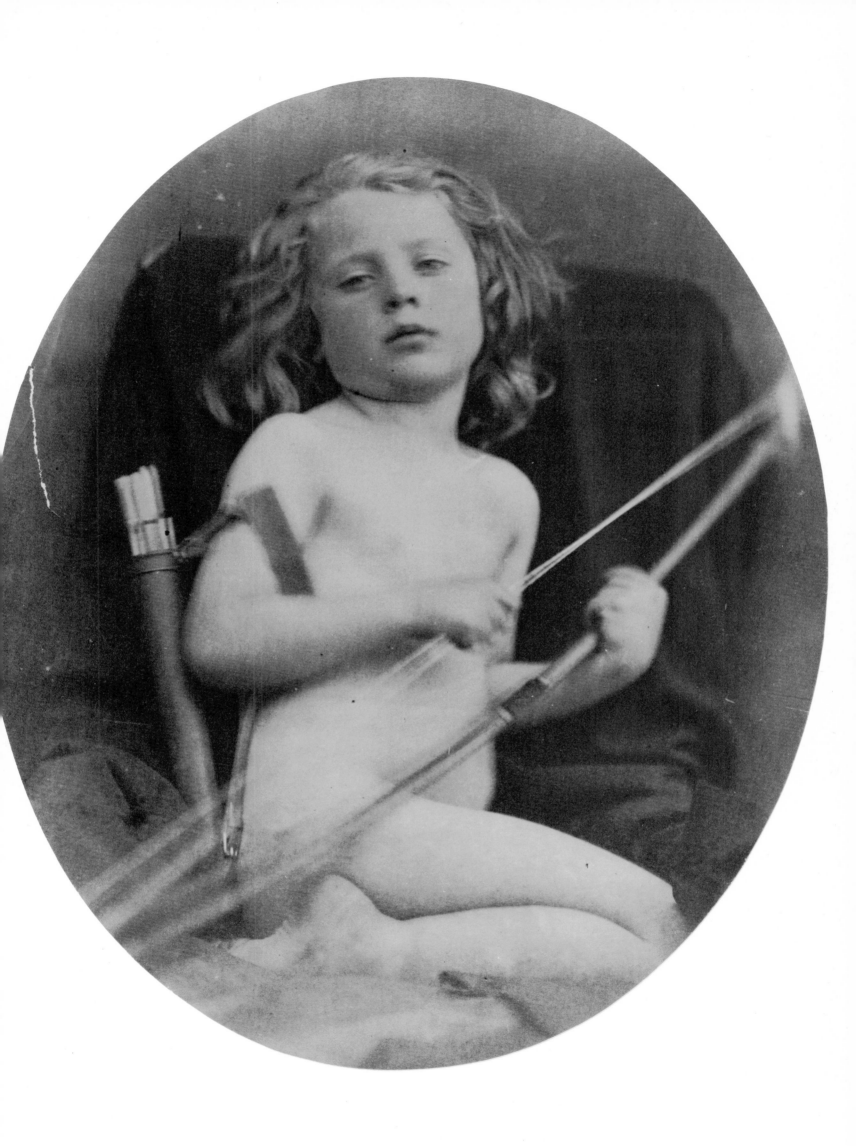

86 *(37)*   J. M. Cameron

Summer Days

c. 1865–6

338 by 256 mm/13.4 by 10.1 in

MAY PRINSEP, Freddy Gould, Lizzie Koewen, Mary Ryan (left to right).
   Mary Ryan was the semi-adopted daughter of Julia and Charles Hay Cameron. She married Henry Cotton (later knighted) of the Indian Civil Service.

87 *(16)*   J. M. Cameron

Lizzie Koewen

c. 1865

186 by 147 mm/7.3 by 5.8 in

88 *(80)*   O. G. Rejlander

Maids drawing water at Freshwater

1864

153 by 106 mm/6.0 by 4.2 in

89 *(55)* J. M. Cameron

Devotion

1865

244 by 213 mm/9.6 by 8.4 in

MARY HILLIER with Archie Cameron, aged two years and three months. Archie was the son of Eugene, eldest son of Julia and Charles Hay Cameron.

90 *(69)*   O. G. Rejlander or Lewis Carroll

Isabel Somers-Cocks

c. 1860–3

144 by 110 mm/5.7 by 4.3 in

91 *(112)* Unknown photographer

Possibly Marie Spartali

c. 1870–5

130 by 96 mm/5.1 by 3.8 in

MARIE SPARTALI was a favourite model of both D. G. Rossetti and Mrs Cameron.

92 *(13)*   J. M. Cameron

Possibly Alice Koewen

c. 1864–5

124 by 132 mm/4.9 by 5.2 in

93 *(III)* Unknown photographer

Possibly Marie Spartali

c. 1870–5

133 by 97 mm/5.3 by 3.8 in

94 *(86)*   G. F. Watts?

Madame de l'Étang in old age

Reproduction of a drawing

152 by 113 mm/6.0 by 4.5 in

THÉRÈSE JOSEPHE DE L'ÉTANG (née Blin de Grincourt) was the maternal grand-
mother of the Pattle sisters.

95 *(68)*   O. G. Rejlander

Isabel Somers-Cocks

c. 1860–3

144 by 110 mm/5.7 by 4.3 in

96 *(91)*   Unknown photographer,
possibly Lord Somers

Henry Herschel Hay Cameron, Arthur
Prinsep, ?, Charles Hay Cameron,
Val Prinsep (left to right)

c. 1860

157 by 207 mm/6.2 by 8.1 in

VAL and Arthur were the second and third sons of Thoby and Sarah Prinsep. Val was later to become a somewhat indifferent painter and writer, and is better remembered as the model for George du Maurier's drawings of 'Taffy' in *Trilby*. Arthur became a general in the Bengal Cavalry.

97 *(12)*   J. M. Cameron

Annie Philpot

January 1864

200 by 154 mm/7.9 by 6.1 in

ANNIE was a local Freshwater girl. This image is often inscribed by Mrs Cameron, 'Annie, my first success'. It is interesting to note that, even after so little experiment, Julia Cameron was very aware of the direction she wished to follow. The image is strong and strangely beautiful, yet utterly timeless.

98 *(92)*   Unknown photographer,
possibly Lord Somers

Henry and Charles Cameron

c. 1860

196 by 135 mm/7.8 by 5.4 in

99 *(24)*   J. M. Cameron

John Jackson

c. 1865

225 by 192 mm/8.9 by 7.6 in

DR JOHN JACKSON was the husband of Maria Pattle, to whom this album was dedicated.

100 *(102)* Unknown photographer

School group

c. 1862

146 by 190 mm/5.8 by 7.5 in

101 *(41)*   J. M. Cameron

Detail from *Summer Days* (Pl. 86)

c. 1865–6

128 mm/5.1 in circle

MARY RYAN.

102 *(105)*   Unknown photographer,
possibly O. G. Rejlander

William Bayley

c. 1860–3

165 by 110 mm/6.5 by 4.3 in

103 *(108)*   Unknown photographer

Family group, including William,
H.V., and Adeline Bayley.

c. 1862–5

65 by 84 mm/2.6 by 3.3 in

104 *(70)*   O. G. Rejlander

Unknown girl, possibly
Adeline Somers-Cocks

Freshwater, *c.* 1863–5

210 by 167 mm/8.3 by 6.6 in

ADELINE was the second daughter of Lord and Lady Somers, and later married the
Marquis of Tavistock.

105 *(74)*   Unknown photographer,
possibly Jabez Hughes or O. G. Rejlander

Sir Henry Taylor

c. 1863–5

167 by 120 mm/6.6 by 4.7 in

106 *(65)*   O. G. Rejlander
or Lewis Carroll

Lionel, Emily, Alfred and
Hallam Tennyson (left to right)

c. 1862–4

161 by 138 mm/6.4 by 5.5 in

THIS photograph, taken at Farringford, is certainly one of the most beautiful and intimate images recorded of the Tennyson family.

107 *(103)*   Unknown photographer,
possibly O. G. Rejlander or Lewis Carroll

William Bayley

c. 1860–3

202 by 150 mm/8.0 by 5.9 in

108 *(22)*   J. M. Cameron

Mrs Herbert Duckworth

c. 1865–6

241 by 189 mm/9.5 by 7.5 in

109 *(94)*   Unknown photographer

Stella Duckworth?

c. 1860–5

90 by 56 mm/3.6 by 2.2 in

STELLA was the daughter of Mrs Herbert Duckworth, and Mrs Cameron's great-niece.

110 *(110)*   Unknown artist

Pietà

Reproduction of a painting

142 by 179 mm/5.6 by 7.1 in

111 *(89)*   O. G. Rejlander

Possibly Marie Spartali

c. 1865–8

96 by 76 mm/3.8 by 3.0 in

112 *(33)* J. M. Cameron

Beauty of Holiness

c. 1865–6

190 mm/7.5 in circle

FREDDY GOULD.

113 *(60)*   O. G. Rejlander

Mrs Herbert Duckworth

c. 1863–5

245 by 185 mm/9.7 by 7.3 in

THE inscription dedicates this to Julia Duckworth's mother, Mrs John Jackson.

For Mrs. Jackson
O.G.R.

114 *(81)*   Unknown photographer,
possibly Jabez Hughes or O. G. Rejlander

Sir Henry Taylor

c. 1863–5

184 by 135 mm/7.3 by 5.4 in

115 *(21)*   J. M. Cameron

Mrs Herbert Duckworth

c. 1865–6

222 by 182 mm/8.8 by 7.2 in

116 *(35)*   J. M. Cameron

Sir Henry Taylor

Freshwater, 1864

263 by 210 mm/10.4 by 8.3 in

Sir Henry Taylor

117 *(104)*   O. G. Rejlander
or Lewis Carroll

Virginia Dalrymple

c. 1860–3

171 by 115 mm/6.8 by 4.5 in

VIRGINIA was the daughter of Sophia, Mrs Cameron's youngest sister, and Sir John Dalrymple. She later married Sir Francis Champneys.

118 *(63)*   Unknown photographer,
possibly Jabez Hughes or O. G. Rejlander

Sir Henry Taylor

c. 1863–5

186 by 120 mm/7.3 by 4.7 in

119 *(52)*   J. M. Cameron

A Rembrandt

c. 1866

242 by 200 mm/9.5 by 7.9 in

SIR HENRY TAYLOR.

Index of sitters and presumed sitters

(references are to plate numbers)